God chasers
for teens

Tommy Tenney

Author's note: This book was written using direct quotes and adaptations from my book, *The God Chasers* (Shippensburg, PA; Destiny Image Publishers, 1998).

Destiny Image® Publishers, Inc.
P.O. Box 310
Shippensburg, PA 17257-0310

"Speaking to the Purposes of God for This Generation
and for the Generations to Come"

ISBN 0-7684-2153-5

For Worldwide Distribution
Printed in the U.S.A.

This book and all other Destiny Image, Revival Press, MercyPlace,
Fresh Bread, Destiny Image Fiction, and Treasure House books are available
at Christian bookstores and distributors worldwide.

For a U.S. bookstore nearest you, call 1-800-722-6774.
For more information on foreign distributors, call 717-532-3040.
Or reach us on the Internet:
www.destinyimage.com

god chasers for

Prepare For The Chase

Do you know God?

We think we know where God lives.

We think we know what He likes, and we are *sure* we know what He dislikes.

This is the problem: Even if I learn a lot of facts about you, that doesn't mean that I actually *know* you.

You may know all about pop celebrities in the movies, on television, and in the music industry; you can know everything about their favorite music, their taste in clothes, and who they "love" at the moment; but does that mean that you really *know* them?

We live in the information age when tidbits of gossip pass from mouth to mouth, from paper to paper, and from computer to computer at the speed of light.

It's very possible to spend years gathering facts about someone without ever knowing them personally.

What about God? Do you know a lot about Him or do you really *know* Him? You may know someone who could win a Bible trivia contest but who obviously doesn't know Him. Maybe that describes you! God is beginning to speak to us in ways we can't ignore. Have you sensed Him nudging your heart recently.

"I'm not asking you how much you know about Me. I want to ask you, 'Do you really know Me? Do you really want Me?' "

I heard that voice and everything changed. I was a Christian and a preacher, and I thought I knew a lot about God. But after I heard God ask me these questions, something began to happen to me.

I was about to discover what it means to KNOW the One I had believed in for so long...

chapter 1

The Day I Met Him

It happened at a church in Houston.

I had ministered at this church several times before, but for two weekends in a row we sensed an unusual *hunger* for God in our meetings. My pastor friend asked me to come back for a third weekend, but this time I was in for a surprise.

As I walked into the early morning service and sat down in the front row, the presence of God was in that place so heavily that the air was "thick." You could barely breathe.

The musicians struggled to continue their ministry because their tears got in the way. Music became more difficult to play. Finally, the presence of God hovered so strongly that they couldn't sing or play any longer. The worship leader crumpled in sobs behind the keyboard.

The atmosphere reminded me of the passage in Isaiah 6, where the glory of the Lord filled the temple. I'd read about, and I even dreamed about experiencing it myself, but I'd never understood what it meant for the glory of the Lord to fill a place.

I had sensed God "entering" places and coming nearby, but this time in Houston His presence literally packed itself into the auditorium (even though I was sure the place was filled with all of God that we could take).

Muffled sobs broke through the room and the pastor turned to me and asked, "Tommy, are you ready to take the service?"

I said, "Pastor, I'm just about half-afraid to step up there, because I sense that *God is about to do something.*" Tears were streaming down my face when I said that. I wasn't afraid that God was going to strike me down, or that something bad was going to happen. I just didn't want to interfere and grieve the precious presence that was filling up that room!

My pastor friend said, "I feel like I should read Second Chronicles 7:14, and I have a word from the Lord."

In a flood of tears, I nodded and said, "Go, go."

He stepped up to the clear pulpit in the center of the platform, opened the Bible, and quietly read the gripping passage from Second Chronicles 7:14: "If My people, which are called by My name, shall humble themselves, and pray, and seek My face, and turn from their wicked ways; then will I hear from heaven, and will forgive their sin, and will heal their land."

Then he closed his Bible, held the edges of the pulpit with trembling hands, and said, "The word of the Lord to us is to stop seeking His benefits and seek Him. We are not to seek His hands any longer, but seek His face."

That is when I heard a thunderclap echo through the building.

And what happened next changed me forever.

CHASE GOD IN THE BIBLE

...I saw the Lord seated on a throne, high and exalted, and the train of his robe filled the temple (Isaiah 6: 1b NIV).

...the priests could not stand to minister...for the glory of the Lord had filled the house of God (2 Chronicles 5:14).

And when all the people saw it, they fell on their faces: and they said, The Lord, He is the God; the Lord, He is the God (1 Kings 18:39).

CHASE GOD IN PRAYER

Lord, it all makes sense. When You *really* show up, people will know it. They sure knew it the day You filled that place in Houston. The people who were there say Your presence was thick and heavy, and they were *worshiping You* then just as they did in the Bible. I want You to *really* show up in my life too. I've made up my mind and I'm not going to change it. I'm going to worship You—right here and right now. Fill my life with Your presence. Amen.

NOTES FOR MY CHASE

_____

_____

_____

_____

_____

_____

_____

_____

_____

Catch Phrase

☐ Repeat this throughout your day ☐

*I am a worshiper
Fill MY life with
Your presence.*

chapter 2

Thunder From Heaven

My pastor friend in Houston is no emotional showoff, so I knew something was going to happen when I watched him walk to the platform. He appeared visibly shaky.

God was going to do something; I just didn't know what, or where. I was in the front row, and it could happen behind me or to the side of me. I was so desperate to catch Him that I walked back to the sound booth so I could see whatever happened. I wasn't even sure that it was going to happen on the platform, but I knew something was going to happen.

"God, I want to be able to see whatever it is You are about to do."

My pastor friend stepped up to the clear pulpit in the center of the platform, opened the Bible, and quietly read Second Chronicles 7:14.

Suddenly, I heard what sounded like a thunderclap echo through the building, and the pastor was literally picked up and thrown backward about ten feet!

When he went backward, the pulpit fell forward. The beautiful flower arrangement positioned in front of it fell to the ground, but by the time the pulpit hit the ground, it was already in two pieces. It had split into two pieces almost as if lightning had hit it!

At that instant we could all *feel* the presence of God fill the room.

I quickly stepped to the microphone and said, "In case you aren't aware of it, God has just moved into this place. The pastor is fine." (He was fine, but it was two-and-a-half hours before he could even get up. We knew he was alive because one of his hands trembled once in awhile.)

People began to weep and to cry out, I said, "If you're not where you need to be, this is a good time to get right with God."

I had never seen anything like what happened next. It was crazy. People shoved each other out of the way. They wouldn't wait for the aisles to clear; they climbed over pews, businessmen tore their ties off, and they were literally stacked on top of one another, in the most horribly harmonious sound of repentance you ever heard.

Just the thought of it still sends chills down my back.

When it was time for the 11:00 service to begin, nobody had left the building. The people were still on their faces and, even though there was hardly any music being played at this point, worship was rampant and uninhibited. Grown men were ballet dancing; little children were weeping in repentance. People were on their faces, on their feet, on their knees, but all were in His presence.

There was so much of the presence and the power of God there that people began to feel an urgent need to be baptized in water. I wasn't sure what to do. Two-and-a-half hours had passed, and the pastor had only managed to wiggle one finger at that point. The ushers had carried him to his office.

Meanwhile, all these people were asking me (or anyone else they could find) if they could be baptized. As a visiting minister at the church, I didn't want to assume the authority to tell anyone to baptize these folks, so I sent people back to the pastor's office to see if he would authorize the water baptisms.

I gave one altar call after another, and hundreds of people were coming forward. As more and more people came to me asking about water baptism, I noticed that no one I had sent to the pastor's office had returned. Finally I sent a senior assistant pastor back there and told him, "Please find out what Pastor wants to do about the water baptisms—nobody has come back to tell me yet."

The man stuck his head in the pastor's office, and to his shock he saw the pastor still lying before the Lord, and everyone I had sent there was sprawled on the floor too, just weeping and repenting before God. He hurried back to tell me what he had seen and added, "I'll go ask him, but if I go in that office I may not be back either."

I shrugged my shoulders and agreed with the associate pastor, "I guess it's all right to baptize them." So we began to baptize people as a physical sign of their repentance before the Lord, and we ended up baptizing people for hours.

That continuous "Sunday morning service" lasted until the early morning hours of the next day.

CHASE GOD IN THE BIBLE

The curtain in the temple sanctuary was split into two parts—from the top to the bottom. The earth shook. Large rocks broke apart (Matthew 27:51 GCENT).

When the day of Pentecost came, they were all together in one place. Suddenly, a noise came from the sky. It sounded like a strong wind blowing. This noise filled the whole house where they were sitting (Acts 2:1-2 GCENT).

After the believers prayed, the place where they were meeting shook. They were all filled with the Holy Spirit and they began to speak God's message without fear (Acts 4:31 GCENT).

CHASE GOD IN PRAYER

You are awesome, Lord. You really shook things up at that church in Houston. You've moved in other places before too. If You move into my life, will You shake me up too?

Go ahead. I *want* You to move in my life, Lord. I hope You shake everything in me. Break down anything that keeps me away from You. Make me the way You want me to be. Amen.

NOTES FOR MY CHASE

_____

_____

_____

_____

_____

_____

_____

_____

_____

_____

Catch Phrase

☐ Repeat this throughout your day ☐

Move in my life and shake up everything, Lord!

chapter 3

Beyond the Broken Pulpit

More and more people kept pouring into the church, and since the people from the early service were still there, parking space became a problem. A ball field next door gradually filled with cars parked every which way.

As people drove onto the parking lot, they sensed the presence of God so strongly that some began to weep uncontrollably. They just found themselves driving up onto the parking lot or onto the grass not knowing what was going on.

Some started to get out of their cars and barely managed to stagger across the parking lot. Some came inside the building only to fall to the floor just inside the doors.

The ushers had to literally pull the helpless people away from the doors and stack them up along the walls of the hallways to clear the entrance. Others managed to make it part way down the hallways, and some made it to the foyer before they fell on their faces, calling out to God.

Some people actually made it inside the auditorium, but most of them didn't bother to find seats. They just made for the altar. No matter what they did or how far they made it, it wasn't long before they began to weep and repent.

There wasn't any preaching. There wasn't even any music part of the time. Primarily one thing happened that day: *The presence of God showed up.* When that happens, the first thing you do is the same thing Isaiah did when he saw the Lord high and lifted up. He cried out from the depths of his soul:

"Woe to me!" I cried. "I am ruined! For I am a man of unclean lips, and I live among a people of unclean lips, and my eyes have seen the King, the Lord Almighty" (Isaiah 6:5 NIV).

The instant Isaiah the prophet saw the King of glory, what he used to think was clean and holy now looked like filthy rags. He was thinking, *I thought I knew God, but I didn't know **this much** of God!*

Throughout the day in Houston, people just kept filling the auditorium again and again, beginning with that strange service that started at 8:30 a.m. I finally went to eat at around 4:00 that afternoon, and then came right back to the church building. Many never left until the early morning hours of the next day.

We didn't have to announce our plans for Monday evening. Everybody already knew. Frankly, there would have been a meeting whether we announced it or not. The people simply went home to get some sleep or do the things they had to do, and they came right back *for more*—not for more of men and their programs, but for God and His presence.

Night after night, the pastor and I would come in and say, "What are we going to do?"

"I don't know what to do. What does *He* want to do?"

Sometimes we'd go in and start trying to "have church," but the crying hunger of the people would quickly draw in the presence of God and suddenly *God had us!* In times like that, you realize God doesn't really care about anything you can "do" for Him; He only cares about your answer to one question: *"Do you want Me?"* We've talked, preached, and taught about revival until the Church is sick of hearing about it. That's what I did for a living: I preached revivals—or so I thought. Then God broke out of His box and *ruined everything* when He showed up.

Seven nights a week, for the next four or five weeks straight, hundreds of people a night would stand in line to repent and receive Christ, worship, wait, and pray. What had happened in history, past and present, was happening again.

Then it dawned on me, "God, You're wanting to do this *everywhere.*"

CHASE GOD IN THE BIBLE

When thou saidst, Seek ye my face; my heart said unto thee, Thy face, Lord, will I seek (Psalm 27:8).

"Then you will call upon Me and come and pray to Me, and I will listen to you. You will seek Me and find me when you seek Me with all your heart. I will be found by you," declares the Lord, "and will bring you back from captivity. I will gather you from all the nations and places where I have banished you," declares the Lord, "and will bring you back to the place from which I carried you into exile" (Jeremiah 29:12-14 NIV).

...He rewards those who earnestly seek Him (Hebrews 11:6 NIV).

...He'll reward all people who have longed for His appearance (2 Timothy 4:8b GCENT).

GET CAUGHT!

Experience God's nearness for yourself! You don't have to be in a large meeting or church service: it can happen in your own room or in some other private place. Simply ask God to make Himself real to you and then sit and wait on him. As you wait, the Holy Spirit will bring areas of your life to mind where you need cleansing and forgiveness. Whisper prayers of repentance and let Jesus wash away your sins and sadness. Listen for His voice and rest in His presence. As you leave your meeting with Him, you will feel stronger, fresher, and cleaner deep inside.

NOTES FOR MY CHASE

_____

_____

_____

_____

_____

_____

_____

_____

_____

_____

Catch Phrase

Remind yourself throughout the day that God is with you and *look for Him* in your home, at school, during rest and activity, and every time you meet with Him.

☐ Pause at regular intervals and whisper ☐

I know You are near, and I'm eagerly looking for Your Presence, Lord.

chapter 4
Forget Your Manners!

As far as I can tell, there is only one thing that stops God from moving into every church like He did that Sunday in Houston.

Hunger.

God looks for hungry people, people who really, *really* want Him.

Have you ever seen hungry people? I mean *really hungry* people. If you could come with me on a ministry trip to Ethiopia or travel to some other country where food is scarce, you would see what happens when sacks of rice are brought among *really hungry* people.

Even when we're hungry, most of us will wait patiently in line at a restaurant or in a food line. That is because we are relatively well fed. *Really hungry people* struggling to survive will get so desperate for food that they forget all about having manners.

That's the way the people were that day in Houston. They were so hungry for the *real thing* from God that they literally forgot their manners. They pushed and shoved to get to the front of the church in their desperation for Him.

Everybody whom I can think of in the New Testament record who "forgot their manners" received something from the Lord. They weren't rude for the sake of rudeness; their rudeness was born out of desperation! One desperate woman with an incurable bleeding problem shoved her way through the crowd until she touched the hem of the Lord's garment (see Mt. 9:20-22).

Another persistent non-Jewish woman just kept begging Jesus to deliver her daughter from demons until He did something (see Mt. 15:22-28).

The Bible says something surprising about the Kingdom of Heaven: "...*the violent take it by force*" (see Mt. 11:12). Have you ever felt that kind of violent hunger for God?

Sometimes we try to satisfy our hunger for God by trying to do good, religious things. Everything good, including the things your local church does—from feeding the poor, to rescuing babies at the pregnancy counseling center, to teaching kids in the Sunday school classes—should flow from the presence of God. Our primary motivating factor should be, "We do it because of Him and because it is His heart."

You can get so caught up in being "religious" that you never become spiritual. It doesn't matter how much you pray. (Pardon me for saying this, but you can be lost, not even knowing God, and still have a prayer life.) I don't care how much you know about the Bible, or what you know *about* Him. I'm asking you, "Do you *know Him?*"

I used to pursue the ministry of preaching good sermons and attempting great accomplishments for Him. None of these things are wrong, but they don't satisfy me anymore. Now I'm a God chaser. Nothing matters more than my pursuit of His presence. I'm going after God. What are you pursuing?

CHASE GOD IN THE BIBLE

As the deer pants for streams of water, so my soul pants for You, O God. My soul thirsts for God, for the living God. When can I go and meet with God? (Psalm 42:1-2 NIV)

O God, You are my God, earnestly I seek You; my soul thirsts for You, my body longs for You, in a dry and weary land where there is no water (Psalm 63:1 NIV).

People who are hungry and thirsty for what is right are happy, because they will be filled. (Matthew 5:6 GCENT).

That desperate longing you feel inside is actually your hunger for God. He put it there, and you should know that your hunger can only be satisfied by Him.

In those moments when you feel "hungry" inside, where do you run? Do you run to do some religious

32

activity to make you feel better? Do you run to the refrigerator? Do you head to the mall or turn to some addictive substance? *Try running to God!*

GET CAUGHT!

Whenever you feel hunger or inner emptiness in your heart this week, don't turn to your usual "satisfiers" (such as a snack machine, activity, or entertainment). Use your hunger to *get caught* instead! Become a desperate God Chaser and run into His Presence.

NOTES FOR MY CHASE

_____

_____

_____

_____

_____

_____

Catch Phrase

Right now, right where you are, whisper this prayer to the Lord.

Lord, I'm desperate and hungry for You. I just want to soak in Your Presence until Your nearness satisfies my deepest longings.

□ Repeat the catch phrase to yourself throughout each day □

When I feel empty and hungry I'll chase God until He finds me!

chapter 5

A Puddle of Tears

A man named Edward Miller wrote a book called, *Cry for Me Argentina*. He told the story of 50 students in his Argentine Bible Institute who prayed so hard that he felt God wanted him to suspend classes until God said to begin them again! For 49 days in a row, the students prayed and interceded for Argentina in the Bible school and angels began to visit them.

Dr. Miller told me that he had never seen people weep so hard and so long in prayer. One young man leaned his head against a concrete brick wall and wept until, after four hours, a trail of tears had run down the wall. After six hours had passed, he was standing in a puddle of his own tears!

Those young intercessors wept day after day, and Dr. Miller said it could only be described as unearthly weeping. The students weren't simply repenting for something they had done. The Holy Spirit was calling them to repent for what had happened through others in their city, their region, and in the country of Argentina.

As a result of the prayers of those Argentine students, the people of Argentina began flocking to evangelistic healing services in soccer stadiums that seated 180,000 people, and even the largest stadiums in the nation weren't big enough to contain the crowds.

I believe that when the full measure of the gathered prayers of God's people finally reach a crescendoing echo in His ears, then it becomes too much for Him to wait any longer. He cannot pass by the prayers of the brokenhearted and contrite who seek His face. Finally the day comes when God says from His throne on high, "That's it."

Are you as desperate as the students in Argentina were? Are you willing to raise your voice with others across this nation to cry out to the Lord on behalf of our country?

CHASE GOD IN THE BIBLE

And I sought for anyone among them who would repair the wall and stand in the breach before me on behalf of the land, so that I would not destroy it; but I found no one (Ezekiel 22:30 NRSV).

The hearts of the people cry out to the Lord. O wall of the Daughter of Zion, let your tears flow like a river day and night; give yourself no relief, your eyes no rest. Arise, cry out in the night, as the watches of the night begin; pour out your heart like water in the presence of the Lord. Lift up your hands to Him for the lives of your children, who faint from hunger at the head of every street (Lamentations 2:18-19 NIV).

We don't know how we should pray, but the Spirit helps our weakness. He personally talks to God for us with feelings which our language cannot express. God searches all men's hearts. He knows what the Spirit is thinking. The

Spirit talks to God in behalf of holy people, using the manner which pleases God (Romans 8:26-27).

CHASE GOD IN PRAYER

"God, my heart burns for You and it breaks for the pain of my generation and my entire nation. I cry out to You for my country, but like it says in Romans, I don't really know how to pray! Help me pray. Holy Spirit, pray through me for this nation. Put a passion and a fire for souls in my heart, and ignite me in fervent prayer for people to turn to You Amen."

Map your PRAYER chase

Get a map of your nation then lay your hands on it and pray. Ask God to show you HOW to pray for:

Government leaders.

Every teenager in your city, state, and nation.

Every school in your area.

WHAT GOD SHOWS YOU
ABOUT YOUR NATION

_____

_____

_____

_____

_____

_____

_____

_____

_____

_____

Catch Phrase

☐ Repeat this throughout your day ☐

*Lord, have mercy on my nation
and pour out Your Grace on us.*

chapter 6

Revival at a Police Station

Many years ago, a young God-chasing evangelist named Duncan Campbell was holding revival services in the New Hebrides, some islands just off the English coast. Some officials from that region came to him at 4:00 one morning and said, "Would you please come to the police station? There is a whole score of people here and we don't know what's wrong with them, but we think you might."

As Duncan Campbell walked with the officials to the police station, it was like a plague had come on the village. People were weeping and praying behind every haystack and every door. Men were kneeling on the street corners and ladies and children in their night-gowns were huddled around each other in their open doorways weeping and crying.

When the evangelist finally reached the police station, he found scores of people crying out to the police, "What is wrong?" The people felt like they had done something very bad and that they were guilty, and they didn't know enough about God to realize that it was Him. The only thing they knew to do was to go to the police station and confess their wrongdoing.

The police didn't have the answer, but Duncan Campbell did. He stood on the steps of the police station early that morning and preached the simple gospel message of Jesus Christ. The people repented to God for their sins and an awesome revival came to that place.

That's the kind of revival I long to see—one that sweeps communities and cities and nations into God's kingdom. There is only one thing that can bring revival to our nation: We need to have God show up. Pray this prayer with me:

"Father, cause a spirit of spiritual violence to grip our hearts. Transform us into warriors of worship. Make us burn with holy passion and a determination to pray with persistence until we break through the heavens. Our cities need You. Our nation needs You, Lord. We are *desperate* for You!

CHASE GOD IN THE BIBLE

If My people, who are called by My name, will humble themselves and pray and seek My face and turn from their wicked ways, then will I hear from heaven and will forgive their sin and will heal their land (2 Chronicles 7:14 NIV).

Repent, then, and turn to God, so that your sins may be wiped out, that times of refreshing may come from the Lord (Acts 3:19 NIV).

So, change your hearts! Come back to God, so that He may wipe out your sins (Acts 3:19 GCENT).

Map your PRAYER chase

You know the drill. Get a map of your nation then lay your hands on it and pray. Ask God to show you HOW to pray for:

A spirit of repentance that people will cause people to cry out to God.

Your school.

People who are in community centers, sports arenas, malls, etc.

WHAT GOD SHOWS YOU
ABOUT YOUR COMMUNITY

_____

_____

_____

_____

_____

_____

_____

_____

_____

_____

Catch Phrase

☐ Repeat this throughout your day ☐

Lord, ambush my
COMMUNITY *with revival!*

chapter 7

Fallen in the Doorway

When God begins to visit in a place or among a people, unusual things start happening simply because He is there. At times His presence often lingers in a place even when no one else is around.

I remember a day that I described earlier when a staff member at the church in Houston went into the sanctuary. It was mid-week and he just went in to tidy up the platform, *but he never came back*. Three hours later somebody noticed that he was gone and some people went looking for him. The light was dim in the sanctuary, and when they turned on the lights, they saw the man lying face down on the platform. He told them later that he had fallen *after stumbling into the cloud of God's presence!*

The pastor of that same church had a brother-in-law who was an atheist. This brother-in-law called and said,

"Look, I'm flying into town. Would you pick me up? I just want to spend a couple of days with you."

The pastor knew something was up, because this brother-in-law had never done that before. The pastor picked him up, and as they drove from the airport, they passed by the church. The pastor said, "That's our church. We just finished some remodeling. You wouldn't want to go in and look at it, would you?"

To his complete surprise, his atheist brother-in-law replied, "Yes, I would."

The pastor pulled into the church parking lot and then unlocked the door to the church building. Then he stepped inside and held the door open for his brother-in-law, and the moment the man's foot touched the floor on the other side of the doorway, he crumpled in a heap and began to weep and cry out, "My God, help me! I'm not ready for this. I don't know how to do this! What am I going to do?"

Then he grabbed the pastor and said, "Tell me how to get saved right now!" So this pastor led his brother-in-law to the Lord right there while he was sprawled half-in and half-out of the building.

Later, the pastor asked him, "What happened to you?" He said, "I don't know how to explain it. All I know is that when I was outside the building I was an atheist and I didn't believe that God existed. But when I stepped across that doorway, I met Him and I knew it was God. I knew I had to get right, and I felt horrible about my life." Then he added, "It just took all the strength out of me."

That man was touched by the power of God!

CHASE GOD IN THE BIBLE

For the kingdom of God is not a matter of talk but of power (I Corinthians 4:20 NIV).

Because the kingdom of God is not talk, but real power (I Corinthians 4:20 GCENT).

He [the unbeliever] will bow down his face and begin to worship God, confessing: "God is really among you!"
(I Corinthians 14:25b GCENT)

GET THE picture

Get a picture of your church, or a church pamphlet of some kind, lay your hands on it and pray. Ask God to show you HOW to pray for:

Your pastors and leaders.

God's will in the services.

The power of God to be there!

WHAT GOD SHOWS YOU
ABOUT YOUR CHURCH

_____

_____

_____

_____

_____

_____

_____

_____

_____

_____

_____

Catch Phrase

☐ Repeat this throughout your day ☐

I pray for my CHURCH.

chapter 8

Touched by the Power

Have you ever scraped your feet across the carpet on a fresh cold day and then touched someone? You probably shocked them with a tiny spark of static electricity. Electricity generated by two feet on a carpet generates enough power to produce a little spark, but generators powered by turbines produce enought raw power to light up a city!

The power of God comes in different forms and quantities as well. When He touches you with the anointing, He may release enough power to produce a little twinge. On the other hand, His glory may overwhelm you with so much intensity that you can't stand in His presence!

I love to read about and study the lives of God Chasers who went before us who knew the *power* of

God. One of them was William Seymour, an African-American man remembered for his role in a great revival that shook the world from a small meeting place on Azusa Street in Los Angeles, California.

Bro. Seymour conducted all-night prayer meetings with other desperate God Chasers and often stuck his head in the apple crate he used as a makeshift pulpit. God's power descended on those meetings with such intensity that it transformed the lives of men and women of many different races. The news about God's presence (and the fire it ignited) spread around the world.

Smith Wigglesworth is another famous God Chaser from the past who walked in the power of God. One pastor began to pray with Mr. Wigglesworth, and he was determined to stay in the prayer room with him. In the end, he finally had to crawl out of the room on his hands and knees, saying, "It was too much of God." Wigglesworth carried the power of God with him wherever he went and many dramatic miracles occurred through his ministry. I call this having a "divine radiation zone."

At times, God's glory flowed in His churches so much that His people had to be careful in area restaurants. One group bowed their heads to say a simple prayer over their meal. When they looked up, they saw waitresses and other customers around them weeping uncontrollably and saying, *"What is it with you people?"*

These things happen when the residue or overflow of God's presence in a person's life creates a divine radiation zone of the manifest presence of God that affects people who are near them. People *notice* individuals who walk in supernatural power. It was the manifest presence of God in the lives of Peter and John that caused the religious elite to say, "They have been with Jesus" (see Acts 4:13).

I don't know about you, but I am tired of blending into the lifeless décor of the uninspired and passionless masses. God wants to see more passionate God Chasers who will walk in His love and power and bring glory to His name.

Make your decision and settle the issue in your heart: "I will pursue the presence of God in my life and I won't stop until I land at His feet."

CHASE GOD IN THE BIBLE

The Jewish leaders saw that Peter and John were not afraid to speak. They were amazed because they understood that the two men had no education or training. Then they realized that Peter and John had been with Jesus (Acts 4:13 GCENT).

CHASE GOD IN PRAYER

"I'm hungry for You and I'm passionate about Your love, Lord. But I also realize that Your power "rubs off" on me. If it brings glory to You, then fill me up and cover me with your manifest presence. Let Your 'divine radiation zone' supernaturally affect and transform the people around me! I want people to look at me and *know* I've been with You, Lord! Amen."

GET THE picture

Lay your hands on pictures of your loved ones and ask God to show you How to pray for:

Your parents and siblings.

God's protection and blessing on your family.

A "divine radiation zone" of God's power in your home and life that will surround you and affect everyone around you.

WHAT GOD SHOWS YOU
ABOUT YOUR FAMILY

_____

_____

_____

_____

_____

_____

_____

_____

_____

Catch Phrase

☐ Repeat this throughout your day ☐

Radiate from me and MY FAMILY as I seek your face Lord.

chapter 9

Grocery Store Line-Up

Time and again we ask one another, "Why can't I win my friends to the Lord? Why aren't my family members interested in God?"

My blunt answer may shock you, but the truth often hurts. Could it be that *people aren't interested in your God because you don't have enough of the presence of God in your life?*

God's presence makes everything else crumble in comparison. Without it, you will be just as pale and lifeless as everybody else around you. Without His presence, you will be "just another somebody" to those around you no matter what you do.

I want to get so close to God that when I walk into secular and public places, people will meet Him. They may not know that I'm there, but they will definitely know that *He* is there. I want to be so saturated with

God's presence that when I take a seat on a plane, everyone near me will suddenly feel uncomfortable if they're not right with God—even though I haven't said a word. I'm not interested in condemning or to convicting them; I just want to carry the fragrance of my Father with me.

My wife was standing in line to pay for some purchases at a store during God's visitation in Houston when a lady tapped her on the shoulder. She turned around to see who it was and found a total stranger weeping unashamedly. This lady told Jeanie, "I don't know where you've been, and I don't know what you've got. But my husband is a lawyer and I'm in the middle of a divorce." She began to blurt out her other problems and finally said, "What I'm really saying is, *I need God.*"

My wife looked around and said, "You mean right here?"

She said, "Right here."

My wife just had to ask again, "Well, what about the people in line?"

Suddenly the lady turned to the woman standing in line behind her and said, "Ma'am, is it okay if I pray with this lady right here?"

But that lady was also crying and she said, "Yes, and pray with me too."

———————

Evangelism is the true purpose for the manifestation or noticeable appearance of God's presence in our lives. If we can carry a residue of God's glory, even a faint glow of His lingering presence with us, then we won't have to beg people to come to the Lord. They will run to Him!

From here on, our prayer should be:

"Father, change our lives and change our church so we can produce change in our city. May our hearts burn so passionately for You that Your glory begins to flow out of us to convict and save the lost. Release Your presence through us as You did through Charles Finney when he walked through factories and saw workers drop to their knees under Your glory! May the overflow of Your presence in us cause unsaved people around us to cry out for forgiveness even if no words are spoken. May the evidence of Your presence in our lives heal the sick and restore the lame we meet in the streets (see Acts 5:15). Let Your presence so saturate us that unsaved guests who enter our homes or come around us feel the need to repent and commit their lives to You. We hunger and thirst for Your presence and power in our lives!"

CHASE GOD IN THE BIBLE

But in your hearts set apart Christ as Lord. Always be prepared to give an answer to everyone who asks you to give the reason for the hope that you have. But do this with gentleness and respect (1 Peter 3:15 NIV).

Make a special holy place in your hearts for Christ, the Lord. Always be ready to give an answer of defense to anyone who asks you why you have hope inside you (1 Peter 3:15 GCENT).

People began to bring their sick into the streets. They put their sick on little beds and mattresses for Peter's shadow to touch them when he came by (Acts 5:15 GCENT).

CHASE GOD IN PRAYER

Write the names of three people you know personally who need Jesus. Pray for them and ask God to prepare you for the next time you meet with them. Ask God to saturate you with His presence so your life will illuminate the need in their lives. Pray. "Jesus, let them see You in me."

_____

_____

_____

Catch Phrase

Everyone hopes to make some kind of lasting mark on the world. *You can make a difference* by carrying the glory of God with you wherever you go. Be filled with His glory this week and allow Him to shine through you into the lives of others. Don't just leave "tracts." Leave divine tracks... leave a lasting impression of Jesus' love in everyone you meet.

God Chasers leave God's tracks.

chapter 10

No More Bless-Me Clubs

My life really began to change the day the Lord told me, *"Son, the services that I like, and the services that you like, are not the same."*

That is when I realized that we often come to church to "get something" from God, when the Bible tells us over and over again to "minister unto the Lord." We spend so much time trying to make people happy and comfortable at church that we neglect our first priority—making sure that God feels welcome and honored in our meetings. We seem to be more interested in services with a "high entertainment index" than in divine encounters with a high "God index."

I began to wonder if we ask God for His presence, but what we really want are His "presents." We want His divine healings, supernatural giftings, and all the miraculous things He can do; but do we really want to honor Him?

The last time I read Psalm 103:1, it said, "Bless the *Lord*, O my soul." It does not say, "O my Lord, bless *my* soul."

Most of the time when we come to church we tell God, "Touch me, bless me, Father," and we make church into "bless me clubs." The truth is that you don't need to worry about having blessings if you spend time with the Blesser!

My ministry requires me to travel quite often, and when I come home to my family, I don't get very excited when my children meet me at the door asking: "What did you bring me, Dad? Did you get me anything?"

I realize that is normal for children, but what I really want is for my kids to sit down and talk to me, with no thoughts about what gift I've tucked into my suitcase.

Father God wishes for the same thing. God chasers want nothing less than God! Nothing can take the place of His presence, not even the "things of God" or the "blessings of God" or the "gifts of God" will satisfy *our hunger for God Himself.*

A God Chaser just wants Him!

CHASE GOD IN THE BIBLE

[Jesus said:] "So, don't worry, thinking to yourself, 'What will we eat?' or, 'What will we drink?' or, 'What will we wear?' People without God put all these things first. Your heavenly Father knows you need all these things. So, put first God's kingdom and what is right. Then all the things you need will be given to you (Matthew 6:31-33 GCENT).

CHASE GOD IN PRAYER

"I'm sorry, Lord. Please forgive me for all the times I came to You just to ask for things. You are my Heavenly Father and I just want to tell You that I love You. There is no prayer request and no want list of stuff I want from You. I've come just to spend some time with You. I love You, Lord."

NOTES FOR MY CHASE

_____

_____

_____

_____

_____

_____

_____

_____

_____

_____

Catch Phrase

Seek the Blesser, not the blessing! Seek His face, not His hands! Don't just get excited about what God has for you; be excited about HIM.

Lord, I want Your PRESENCE more than Your presents.

chapter 11

Don't "Date" God

There is something in us that makes us afraid of the commitment that comes with real intimacy with God. For one thing, intimacy with God requires *purity*. The days of fun and games in the Church are over. What do I mean by "fun and games"?

If your definition of fun is "low commitment and lots of thrills and chills," then all you've ever wanted to do is "date God." You've just been wanting to get in the backseat with Him.

God is tired of us coming to get our thrills from Him without putting on the ring of commitment! Some people are more in love with the "goose bumps" than with His glory! They're addicted to the anointing, liking the feeling of being blessed, receiving the "gifts" like a religious "gold-digger," happy with chocolates, flowers, and jewelry. The last time I checked, He was still looking for a bride, not a girlfriend; one who will "stick" with Him.

I'm afraid that many people in the Church have simply approached God to get what they can from Him without committing anything in return. God is saying to His Church, "I don't want that. Let's pledge ourselves to each other."

We've often placed the cart before the horse. We seek revival without seeking *Him*. Leaders in the Church have written countless books on how to grow churches, but sometimes the underlying message there is, "This is how to grow churches without a relationship with Him."

Most Christians in North America are "hothouse Christians" who bloom as long as they are kept in a protected and carefully controlled environment far from fear, distress, or persecution. "God forbid that it should 'cost' us something to speak the name of Jesus."

But time and again, we have seen that if you take hothouse Christians out of their protected environment and put them into the real world where the wind of adversity blows and the rain of sorrow falls; if they have to endure the hot sun and the drought it brings, then they discover that they never developed a root system in the hothouse. So they wither and say, "I'm just not cut out for this!"

If it takes the "perfection of environment" to prove the presence of God in someone's life, then my guess is that the persecuted Christians just don't have God. How can they? They don't have Bible seminars; they don't have choirs or the latest worship music. They don't have air conditioning, ushers, nurseries, electronic paging systems, carpeted sanctuaries, or staff counselors. Their worship environment is terrible.

If they get caught having church, they must pay a terrible price. I read an account of a group of Chinese Christians who were caught holding a church service. The officials placed a horse trough in the middle of town and forced every man and woman in that congregation to urinate into it. Then they drowned the pastor in it, right in front of their eyes!

Do you know what happened? The church congregation doubled in two weeks, and it sure wasn't because of their nice sanctuary or dynamic worship team.

These kinds of believers don't gauge their relationship with God by how things are going with their bank account, or by how much "fun" they've had during church activities. They have joined Paul by saying: "My life doesn't matter. The most important thing is that I finish the race—the work which the Lord Jesus gave me to do, telling people the Good News about God's gracious love" (Acts 20:24 GCENT). This is the confession of people in love and in intimate communion with their Maker.

The games are over. God is calling you.

CHASE GOD IN THE BIBLE

What was planted on rocky soil is the person who hears the message and accepts it with gladness right away. However, he does not have deep roots in himself; he doesn't last long. When, because of the message, trouble or persecution comes, he soon gets discouraged and gives up. That which was planted among the thorny weeds is the one who hears the message, but the worries of this age and deceiving riches choke out the message. It never produces fruit (Matthew 13:20-22 GCENT).

"Not everyone who says to Me, 'Lord! Lord!' will enter the kingdom of heaven. Only the person who does what My heavenly Father wants will enter it" (Matthew 7:21 GCENT).

You must love the Lord your God from all your heart, from all your soul, from all your mind, and from all your strength (Mark 12:30 GCENT).

CHASE GOD IN PRAYER

"Jesus, it isn't enough for me to just call You Lord, I want You to *be* my Lord! Fun and games and playing church don't satisfy me anymore. I'm hungry for You and I'm ready to make an all-out, total commitment to You."

WHAT GOD SHOWS YOU
ABOUT YOUR CHURCH

_____

_____

_____

_____

_____

_____

_____

_____

_____

_____

_____

Catch Phrase

☐ Repeat this throughout your day ☐

I'm commited. I'm yours, Lord.

chapter 12

It Will Cost Your Life

I know a pastor in Ethiopia who was ministering in a church service when men from the Communist government there interrupted the meeting and said, "We are here to stop you from having church."

They had already done everything they knew to do but without success, so that day they grabbed the pastor's three-year-old daughter and literally threw her out the second-story window of the building while everybody watched.

The Communists thought that would stop the service, but the pastor's wife went down to the ground floor, cradled her dead baby in her arms, and returned to her seat on the front row and worship continued. As a result of this kind of faithfulness, 400,000 devout believers would boldly show up for that pastor's Bible conferences in Ethiopia.

One time my father, a national leader in a Pentecostal denomination in America, was talking with this pastor. He knew that this pastor lived in horrible poverty in Ethiopia, and he made the mistake of showing a little bit of what he thought would be gracious sympathy. He told this Ethiopian pastor, "Brother, we pray for you in your poverty."

This humble man turned to my father and said, "No, you don't understand. *We pray for you in your prosperity.*" That took my father aback, but the Ethiopian pastor explained, "We pray for you Americans because it is much harder for you to live at the place God wants you to live in the midst of prosperity, than it is for us in the midst of our poverty."

The greatest trick the enemy has used to rob the American Church of its vitality has been the "lollipop of prosperity." I am not against prosperity. Be as prosperous as you want to be, but pursue Him instead of the prosperity. You see, it is very easy to begin chasing

God and wind up chasing something else! Don't be like that. Be a God chaser. Period.

One of the first steps to real revival is to recognize that you are in a state of decline. This isn't an easy task in our professed prosperity, but we need to say, "We're in decline; we're not in the best of times." Ironically, we find ourselves in the odd situation of matching the famous line from *A Tale of Two Cities* by Charles Dickens, "It was the best of times, it was the worst of times."

It might be the best of times economically, but on the whole, the Church is not riding a wave of spiritual prosperity. How long has it been since your shadow healed anybody? How long has it been since your mere presence in a room caused people to say, "I've got to get right with God"?

The bottom line of the whole matter is simple: Are you willing to pay the cost of becoming a God chaser?

Salvation is a free gift, but God's glory will cost you everything.

It will cost your life.

CHASE GOD IN THE BIBLE

The person who loves his father or mother more than Me is not worthy of Me. The person who loves his son or daughter more than Me is not worthy of Me. The person who does not accept his cross and follow Me is not worthy of Me. The person who finds his life will lose it, but the person who gives his life away because of Me will find it. (Matthew 10:37-39 GCENT).

You don't belong to yourselves. You were bought; you cost something. Use your body to give glory to God! (I Corinthians 6:19b-20 GCENT)

So, the life which I now live is not really me—it is Christ living in me! I still live in my body, but I live by faith in the Son of God. He is the one who loved me; He sacrificed Himself for me (Galatians 2:20 GCENT).

CHASE GOD IN PRAYER

"Lord, it looks as if You are asking me to give up my whole life. That means my dreams, ambitions, and even my daily decisions wouldn't be long to me anymore.

"I'm not sure about all of this, but *I know I want my life to count* for something that matters. I don't want to just exist and then die. And the only way my life will ever really matter is if I let You live through me.

"Help me, Lord. I'm desperate for You, and my pursuit of Your presence has brought me to the end of myself. Take control of my life and fill me with Your presence."

NOTES FOR MY CHASE

_____

_____

_____

_____

_____

_____

_____

Catch Phrase

☐ Repeat this throughout your day ☐

My life is not my own. I've been bought with a price—now I live to follow Him and share His presence with everyone I meet.

chapter 13

World Changers

My definition of revival is when God's glory breaks out of the four walls of our churches to flow through the streets of the city.

Revival of historical proportions in modern times would be when God invades the shopping malls on Friday night. I want to see every mall association be forced to hire full-time chaplains just to handle the crowds of people they find weeping under conviction each shopping day. I want to see citywide calls for volunteer ministers just to handle the flood of people who get convicted of their sins when they pass through the town. (Security guards know what to do with shoplifters, but would they know what to do with people who come up to them in distress because they've been convicted of their sin?) I'm ready to see it *now*!

God's glory is destined to cover the whole earth (see Num. 21:14; Hab. 2:14). It has to start somewhere. Jesus said that from our bellies, from our innermost being, rivers of living water will flow (see Jn. 7:38). Why not in *your* church, town, or city?

God wants wants us to be so saturated with His glory that we carry His presence with us everywhere we go in this life. This may be the only way the unspeakable glory of God will find its way to the schools, shopping malls, hair style salons, and grocery stores of our nation. It has to start with somebody. Why not *you*?

We want God to change the world but we must realize that change must begin in us first. If we will let Him, He will make us—all of us—into what He needs us to be.

You might say, "But how can He change me?"

Well, isn't He the Creator who stepped out on the balcony of Heaven and scooped out the seven seas with the palms of His hands? Wasn't it God who pinched the earth to make the mountains? Wasn't He the One who turned fishermen into world-changers and hated tax collectors into fearless preachers? He's done it before, and He'll do it again! It has to begin sometime. Why not *now*?

The way we are changed is *by spending time with Him.*

God is calling you to come close. Dare to answer His call and let the Lord pull you so close that you feel as if you are breathing the very air of Heaven.

Often I see the aisles of churches filled with people who have climbed into the lap of the Father. When I see them hiding their faces underneath benches and pews as they seek the face of God I say, "Yes! This is it! This is the way the world will be changed."

This is the way God's glory is destined to cover the whole earth.

It starts right here and right now. Are you hungry for Him?

CHASE GOD IN THE BIBLE

For the earth will be filled with the knowledge of the glory of the Lord, as the waters cover the sea (Habakkuk 2:14 NIV).

As for me, I will behold thy face in righteousness: I shall be satisfied, when I awake, with thy likeness (Psalm 17:15).

All of us have uncovered faces; we reflect the same glory. It comes from the Spirit of the Lord. With one glory after another, we are being changed to look more like Him (2 Corinthians 3:18 GCENT).

GET CAUGHT!

How do you "chase God"? You spend time in His Presence.

Choose a time and place free of distractions and begin to tell Him how much you love Him. Don't seek His hand—don't bring out your prayer list. He will ask you for it when He is ready.

Allow yourself to love and be loved by Him. It is in His Presence that you will be changed and transformed into the image of Jesus. The more you seek Him, the more You begin to look like Him!

NOTES FOR MY CHASE

_____

_____

_____

_____

_____

_____

_____

_____

_____

Catch Phrase

☐ Repeat this throughout your day ☐

It starts right here
and right now.

chapter 14

FINISH LINES

You have been reading this book by divine appointment. Somewhere, somehow, an unforgettable prayer is being answered today. Perhaps you've avoided this moment until now, knowing you should surrender your life to Jesus. It could be that you've been a "good Christian" running from the altar of sacrifice that God has placed before you.

Don't run *from* Him. Run *to* Him. Run into His arms with childlike trust and passionate hunger. This is the life of a God chaser. This is the goal and the reason for our pursuit—to live life in the Father's arms. This is what it means "to live and move and have our very being in Him" (see Acts 17:28).

Race into His presence. Give Him your fears, your worries, and all of your problems. Trust Him with your dreams and your hopes. Lay back and rest in Him knowing that He loves you and cares for you.

Nothing else is needed; nothing else is necessary. Become as a little child who lays down his toys to crawl into the Father's lap to seek His face. This is the place where you will find the peace you've always longed for. He is the only one who can satisfy your hungry heart.

The famous God chaser, Paul the Apostle said this:

I press on to win what Christ Jesus won for me. Brothers, I don't think I've already won it, but I'm doing one thing: I am reaching out—forgetting about what is behind me. I am pressing on toward the goal to win the prize to which God called me. It is above in Christ Jesus (Philippians 3:12-14 GCENT).

The mark, the goal, the prize—is Jesus. He is the One we are chasing, and He will not frustrate us. God

will allow Himself to be caught by us. As a father playing tag with his child allows himself to be caught by the
laughing, loving child, so too will the heavenly Father
allow Himself to be caught. In fact, as you chase Him,
He will turn and catch you!

Paul, champion God Chaser, wrote this, according to
the King James Version:

*I follow after, if that I may apprehend that for which also
I am apprehended of Christ Jesus* (Philippians 3:12b).

Paul caught Him and so can you! Join the company
of God chasers!

The "chase" is on….

NOTES FOR MY CHASE

_____

_____

_____

_____

_____

_____

_____

_____

_____

Catch Phrase

Once you have seen His glory, nothing in this world will ever satisfy you. Nothing this life offers compares to being in His Presence. The Bible says that we live and move and have our being in Him (see Acts 17:28). Live that way! Whether you face a crisis, a problem, or are enjoying moments of sweet communion with Him; make this declaration in every situation...

I am a God Chaser.

GOD*Chasers.network*

GodChasers.network is the ministry of Tommy and Jeannie Tenney. Their heart's desire is to see the presence and power of God fall—not just in churches, but on cities and communities all over the world.

How to contact us:

By Mail:

GodChasers.network
P.O. Box 3355
Pineville, Louisiana 71361
USA

By Phone:

Voice: 318.44CHASE (318.442.4273)
Fax: 318.442.6884
Orders: 888.433.3355

By Internet:

E-mail: GodChaser@GodChasers.net
Website: www.GodChasers.net

god chasers for God

Run With Us!

Become a GodChasers.network Monthly Revival Partner

Godchasers are people whose hunger for Him compels them to run—not walk—towards a deeper and more meaningful relationship with the Almighty! For them, it isn't just a casual pursuit. Traditional Sundays and Wednesdays aren't enough—they need Him everyday, in every situation and circumstance, the good times and bad. Are you a GodChaser? Do you believe the body of Christ needs Revival? If my mandate of personal, National and International Revival is a message that resonates in your spirit, I want you to prayfully consider Running with us! Our Revival Partners fuel GodChasers.network to bring the message of unity and the pursuit of His presence around the world! And the results are incredible, yet humbling. As a Revival Partner, your monthly seed becomes the matches we use to set Revival fires around the globe.

For your monthly support of at least thirty dollars or more, I will send you free, personal fuel each month. This could be audio or videotapes of what I feel the Lord is saying that month. In addition, you will receive discounts on all of our ministry resources. Your Revival Partner status will automatically include you in invitation-only gatherings where I will minister in a more intimate setting.

I rely on our Revival Partners to intercede for the ministry in prayer and even minister with us at GodChaser gatherings around the country. I love to sow seed in peoples' lives and have learned that you can't out give God, He always multiplies the seed! If we give Him something to work with, there's no limit how many He can feed, or how many Revival fires can be started!

Will you run with us every month?

In Pursuit,

Tony Tenney

Tommy Tenney

Become a Monthly Revival Partner by calling or writing to:

Tommy Tenney/GodChasers.network
P.O. Box 3355
Pineville, Louisiana 71361-3355
318.44CHASE (318.442.4273)

Other **God Chaser** Gift Books
Available Everywhere
You Are a God Chaser If... 0-7684-2164-0
God Chasers for Kids 0-7684-2165-9

For a complete list of our titles,
visit us at www.destinyimage.com
Send a request for a catalog to:

Destiny Image® Publishers, Inc.
P.O. Box 310
Shippensburg, PA 17257-0310